THE Butterfly Strategy

VAL ROSKENS TEWS

Copyright ©2026   Published by Val Roskens Tews

The author and/or publisher does not guarantee that anyone following these suggestions, ideas, or tips in this book will become successful. The author does not guarantee results and accepts no responsibility for any loss or damage arising from use of the information in this book. LinkedIn is the registered trademark of LinkedIn Corporation or its affiliates. The use of the LinkedIn trademark in connection with this product does not signify any affiliation with or endorsement by LinkedIn Corporation or its affiliates.

All rights reserved. No part of this publication may be reproduced, distributed, or transmitted in any form or by any means, electronic or mechanical, including photocopying, recording, or any information storage and retrieval system, without the prior written permission of the publisher. Requests to the publisher for permission should be addressed to val@butterflycopywriting.com.

ISBN 979-8-9941999-0-9 (Paperback)
ISBN 979-8-9941999-1-6 (EBook)

Book Design & Layout: Toni Serofin, Sanserofin Studio

READER BONUS

Your Social Media Impact Trifecta

Connecting, commenting, and posting content are important individual actions in your social media strategy, but it's the combination of all three that creates the biggest impact — transforming your efforts into a community of potential clients, readers, and business friends. That's where Your Social Media Impact Trifecta comes in.

This free guide will show you how to:

- Find like-minded people to connect with.
- Spark conversations, beginning with commenting.
- Create authentic content that expands your community, online and off.

 Scan the QR code to download a free copy of *Your Social Media Impact Trifecta* — the perfect companion to the book in your hands.

Dedication

This book is dedicated to three special coaches whose mentorship and guidance have been invaluable.

ILISE BENUN   Thank you for believing in me when I didn't believe in myself. Your invitation to share my story as part of your 21-Day LinkedIn Challenges planted the seeds that have bloomed into this book, a guide, and a masterclass. You gave me the confidence to show up and discover amazing people on LinkedIn. I am grateful for you!

LISA MULLIS   Thank you for your encouragement and direction as I discovered new ways to share my mission. You helped me enhance my messaging by providing gentle feedback while still allowing me to be *me*, and to show up authentically. I am grateful for you!

JESSICA ANDERSEN   Thank you for your invaluable assistance in getting this story to its final form. Your suggestions wonderfully enhanced my original. Your encouragement throughout this process is most appreciated! You have an incredible gift and I'm blessed that you shared it with me! Thank you! I am grateful for you!

Our job as people of impact is to build bridges of connection with those around us. If we do it right, people want to walk across those bridges, back and forth, to join one another.

Do you spend more effort shouting across the divide or building a bridge?

– Tim Brand

Contents

Foreword   xi

Introduction   1
Why LinkedIn?   3
The Importance of the 3Cs   5
Where to Begin?   8

PART 1
Your Transformation Superpowers   13
The Butterfly Represents the 3Cs   14
    of Your LinkedIn Strategy
Connecting   18
Commenting   24
Content   30
Your Social Media Impact Trifecta   34

PART 2
Content Creation   39
Creating an Article   40
Five Post Ideas with Examples   46

PART 3

Butterfly Strategy Principles	65
Your Proverbial Scales	65
Your Content Diet	66
Flying "Cold"	67
Making Time	68
Your Ultraviolet Message	68
Choose to Be a Butterfly by Using Your Transformation Superpowers!	70

PART 4

Glossary of Terms	75
Acknowledgments	79
About the Author	81
Endnotes	83

Foreword

Conversations about social media often swing between hype and overwhelm. We're inundated with advice about posting consistently, chasing algorithms, and going viral in the hope that potential buyers will notice. Yet there's very little guidance on how to leverage content and form the kind of relationships that sustain a business. That's what makes *The Butterfly Strategy* so valuable: it clears away the noise and offers a simple, human-centered path forward.

With Val's background in journalism, public relations, and content strategy, she understands both the technical and the human sides of communication. But what sets her apart is the heart she brings to her work. She believes in building genuine relationships, not transactional ones, and she models that belief in her own presence online. If you've ever felt lost in the mechanics of social media, her voice in these pages will feel like a trusted companion pointing you back to what matters most: people.

Val uses the butterfly metaphor in each chapter to show that connection leads to transformation, growth is gradual, and social platforms are powered by people rather than technology. Her framework of the "3Cs" — connecting, commenting, and content — is simple, but stellar: together they form the foundation of your impact on social media.

Instead of vague encouragement to "engage more" or "be authentic," Val provides clear, tactical guidance and examples that make each of the 3Cs easy to implement. She shows you what to say in a comment, how to approach new connections, and how to create purposeful content without burning yourself out. The strategies in these pages are ones you can put into practice immediately.

Social media can feel intimidating, especially for those who worry about saying the wrong thing or not having enough time to devote to working the system. Val doesn't dismiss those concerns; she names them and offers ways through them. Her writing is a reminder that you don't have to be perfect to be effective — you only need a willingness to connect, to share, and to keep showing up.

As you turn the pages ahead, I encourage you not only to read but to experiment. Try out the exercises, adapt the examples, and notice the shift when you approach social media as an opportunity to build community instead of a burden to manage. *The Butterfly Strategy* is

Foreword

more than a system; it's an invitation to step out of the chrysalis of hesitation and take flight with more clarity, confidence, and joy.

– Lisa Mullis

Introduction

Before a butterfly can take flight for the first time, a metamorphosis must take place. In that dark, confined space, growth is driving change. It takes time, and it's not flashy — it's all happening behind the scenes until the glorious transformation is complete.

Inside the stillness, yet unseen, the caterpillar becomes a butterfly. And when it emerges, it starts a whole new life.

If you have been using LinkedIn (or another social media platform) for a while, it might feel like you are in the "caterpillar stage" — in a chrysalis in the dark, with seemingly nothing happening.

To reach the next stage, you need a supportive environment. The cocoon of social media looks different from platform to platform, but three elements can help you thrive in any of them and emerge a butterfly: strategic connecting, commenting, and content creation. Together, these elements will help you build a *community* of people who will support and encourage you.

NOTE: LinkedIn is my social media platform of choice, so I reference it throughout this book. The principles of the *Butterfly Strategy*, however, can apply to other social media platforms.

If you are currently using social media strictly to drive sales or conversions, and you're seeing lackluster results, remember why the platform was designed: for people to connect! Before getting a client from posting content, you need to first create a community of people who support and encourage you, and whom *you* can support and encourage. Building a positive community is what makes the difference in running a successful business, in building a hype team for the book you've written, in finding "your people." But that community doesn't just appear out of thin air the day you sign up to the platform — it only develops from building relationships.

Just one comment can lead to a conversation which can lead to a friendship or a business relationship — in my experience, sometimes both!

On LinkedIn, anyone is a potential *business friend*. While some may become clients, most will not. The ones who don't can still be a valuable source of referrals or industry knowledge, or even a sounding board for your brilliant new ideas. These business friends are also the ones who will amplify your voice when you're sharing about your mission, your book, your course, your membership, whatever it is.

How do you cultivate your supportive online community? It's simple: by connecting, commenting, and creating content.

Why LinkedIn?

Here's why being on LinkedIn can make an impactful difference for you and your business.

It's important to build a personal brand that goes beyond your business or your job. *Carrie Bryson*, who is an expert job search strategist, explains it this way:

> "In today's hyper-connected world, your LinkedIn profile is more than a digital résumé — it's your personal brand billboard. Whether you work for a company, a startup, or freelance, one thing remains true: you are your brand.

While promoting your employer is valuable, relying solely on company affiliation can cause your personal identity to fade into the background. Building a strong, authentic LinkedIn presence is a strategic move — whether you're job hunting, networking, or aiming to establish yourself as a thought leader.

Your brand matters more than ever, because when you build your brand around who you are, not just where you work, you create a portable, powerful identity that follows you throughout your career. This is your time to showcase the value and knowledge you bring to your industry and any organization.

Your brand is more than a headline or highlight reel. It's the intersection of your values, voice, strengths, and the perspective only you can offer. It's how people remember you, refer you, and recognize your impact. On LinkedIn, your profile isn't just a placeholder, it's the room where that conversation begins."

Look at LinkedIn as the professional place to start conversations, rather than *just* another social media platform to be on. Focus on establishing *business friendships* rather than likes. Creating a community is where learning, leads, and supportive relationships can happen.

LinkedIn offers networking opportunities that can expand from local to global. It's a place to share challenges, find answers, share celebrations, give encouragement, and find real value.

It's a place where you can share your message and make an impact. Your credibility can be shown through your comments and your thought leadership content. Look at this platform as a space to grow, learn, and to share what you know with others.

The Importance of the 3Cs

When you first start out on social media, you'll probably *connect* with people you already know in real life, such as friends and family. But you'll need to branch out beyond your usual network and build a following. When people "meet" you online for the first time, you need to nurture them to become business friends.

One way to expand your network is by *commenting*: leaving your thoughts on other people's posts as well as responding to comments on your posts. Commenting can lead to deeper conversations, but only if you're proactive about it — yes, you must *ask* for a conversation. (Try offering a "virtual coffee chat," or a getting-to-know-you call.)

Many people, however, start with *content*. They post relentlessly and then wonder why it's "not working." While content is important, if you don't have the supportive connections to view your posts, your content won't be working as hard as it could for you because few will see it. The smaller your community, the smaller your reach — that's just how algorithms work. However, content has a much higher impact after you've connected with someone who is curious about the topics you share, what your values are, and what you believe.

The bottom line is that you need all three to be effective: connecting, commenting, and content.

Connecting can be hard when you are avoiding the sting of rejection. Commenting may be even harder if you're afraid of how your words are perceived. Content creation can also be a challenge if you have writer's block, or if you're in a mindset of posting for the sake of posting.

Introduction

As a small business owner, a coach, or an author, it's crucial that you grow your audience and attract clients without getting stuck in the overwhelm of what to post or how to say it. But you may not know whom to connect with. Once you connect, you may not know what to say in the comments, so you don't say anything.

And if you do know what to say, you want to be consistent, but you may feel there isn't enough time for everything — especially content creation. When you finally do have time, the right words might not come to you easily.

In short, you risk establishing a social media presence that does not truly reflect who you are.

- Are you telling yourself, "I'll post next week"?
- Or waiting for inspiration to tell you what to write?
- Or posting something just to be posting — but it isn't what you really want to say?

Although it's a common place to get stuck, you don't have to stay in the chrysalis of *not* posting, *not* commenting, *not* sharing about your business because you're unsure of what to say or do. You can be successful on social media... because you have transformation superpowers!

Strategic connecting, commenting, and content creation are your transformation superpowers.

What do I mean by transformation? When you share your message via the 3Cs, you are inspiring people to act. You are helping them to change for the better. You are helping people to make a positive impact, whether in their own lives or in others'.

You wrote your book for a reason — that's your message, that's your impact. You're a coach because you know you can help people find specific solutions to their problems. But if the people you serve don't know about your mission, they won't buy your book or hire you as their coach. You need to go public with your message! Someone is waiting to hear it — *they will miss out on a transformation if you don't share it.*

Where to Begin?

Now that you know about the 3Cs, aka your transformation superpowers, how do you put them to work?

The first step is to create a strategy — without one, it's hard to build momentum. If you're expecting to come up

Introduction

with content ideas thanks to "inspiration" alone, or thinking that time will magically appear in your schedule to find new connections, or saving commenting for Sunday afternoon... it probably won't happen.

A strategy allows you to work smarter because you'll have content created, taking the pressure off relying on that "inspiration" or finding that "extra time." A strategy allows your ideas to emerge from the cocoon and become strong because the content is authentic to you. A strategy also keeps you from going in circles, wasting your limited time and attention.

You need to know exactly *what* to implement and *when*. You need a plan with intentional ideas that really reflect who you are and what your message is. That's why I developed the *Butterfly Strategy*.

PART 1

Your Transformation Superpowers

A butterfly shows us what genuine transformation looks like. A caterpillar doesn't have to prove anything before metamorphosis — it just does what comes naturally. That's why authenticity is at the heart of the Butterfly Strategy: when you choose to share from your heart, you kindle a transformation to serve others. With the Butterfly Strategy, you'll be intentional, purposeful, and confident, and you'll effortlessly transform connections into community and potential clients.

If you're still in caterpillar mode, stuck inside your proverbial cocoon, how can you break free? First, you must believe in yourself. Sometimes, it's also necessary to ask for help before you can take flight and serve others.

Remember: strategic connecting, commenting, and content creation are your transformation superpowers to help you make the biggest impact.

Start a ripple effect through creating *connections*. Help your network bloom through positive *commenting*. Transform others by sharing your message through *content*.

The Butterfly Represents the 3Cs of Your LinkedIn Strategy

1 | Body = Connecting

Butterflies create a ripple effect. As they travel from flower to flower, they don't just take in needed nutrients; they also give back through pollination, which helps flowers bloom.

Create a ripple effect by making meaningful connections. Just like a butterfly helps flowers bloom, you can help others thrive through connecting with them, and supporting and encouraging them. While progress might seem slow at first, your efforts to expand your network will compound. The more people who know you, the more people who will meet you — and the more people who will read your book or ask you to become their coach!

2 | Left Wing = Commenting

Help your network bloom through positive commenting.

Think of people's profiles as flowers. You can help them bloom by acknowledging them through commenting. Spark conversations by leaving thoughtful comments on others' posts. Your comments can lead to making business

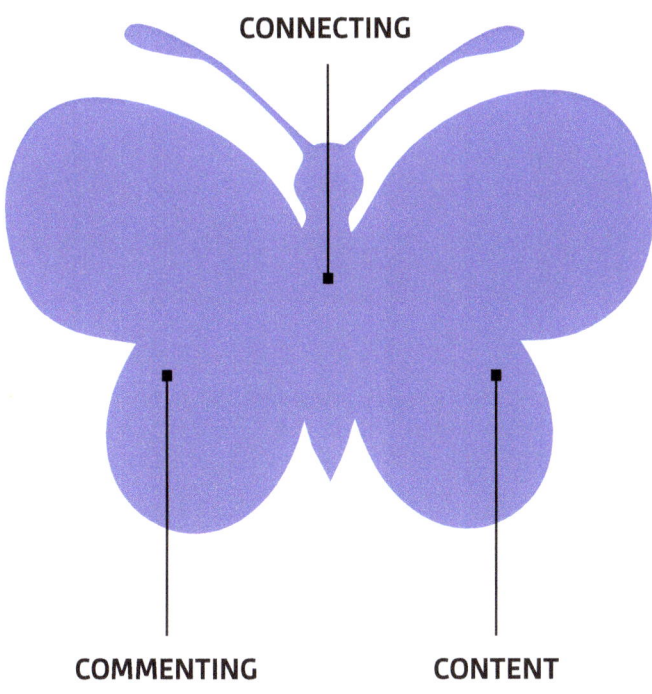

friends — not only with the author of the post but also with incredible people in the comments.

3 | Right Wing = Content

Content creates trust. It's a way of letting the "right" people know they are in the right place.

Transformation begins by sharing your message. Start small by creating "micro content": short posts, each with one main idea. You don't have to post every day — two or three times a week is enough. Whatever cadence you choose, just make sure to be consistent with it, and vary your content with both "business" and "personality" posts.

By *business posts* I mean content about whom you serve and how. You can draw inspiration from everyday life and use it as a metaphor for business or marketing. You can also include case studies and testimonials from clients. For authors, this includes sharing about your book — excerpts, character profiles, themes, and more.

Personality posts, on the other hand, include content about yourself outside of the business sphere. Share about your favorite activity or hobby; for example, I once shared about my baking exploits. If you're used to sharing only the buttoned-up version of yourself online, posting more personal content can feel uncomfortable at first, especially if you are a private person. Remember, you can be vulnerable without dishing the details of your personal life. People want to know who you are offline, how you like to spend your time, and what matters to you outside of business. Although these posts aren't sales-driven, they still serve a purpose: resonating with like-minded people. The more people know you and like you, the more likely they are to trust you when they are ready to make their transformation.

Your Social Media Impact Trifecta

If you read nothing else in this book, please read this! It's the most important part of the Butterfly Strategy, and it's why I wrote this book.

While connecting, commenting, and posting content are each important individual actions in your social media strategy, it's the strategic combination of all three that creates the biggest impact — transforming your efforts into a community of potential clients, readers, and business friends. This is your *Social Media Impact Trifecta*!

Find people you can relate to and connect with them. Start conversations with those new connections, beginning by commenting on their posts. Allow your network to learn about who you are through the content you post. But don't stop there: deepen new connections through thoughtful, intentional commenting, and create content to help establish the "know, like, and trust" factor early on. Leveraging the 3Cs will transform what may have felt like random clicks and likes into meaningful conversations which can lead to new opportunities for your business.

At its core, the Butterfly Strategy is about *people*. People do business with other people. By nurturing positive relationships with your connections on LinkedIn, you'll create a community of people who support you. Those are the people who will amplify your message, read your book when it launches, refer clients to you, and yes — they may even become clients themselves!

Let's take an in-depth look at the 3Cs at work, with tips for each. Be sure to download your free Social Media Impact Trifecta to guide you as you plan out your Butterfly Strategy.

Connecting

While you may be tempted to connect with anyone and everyone to increase the size of your network, concentrate on "who" rather than just the numbers. It's the people who make the difference! You want to create a community of people who support and encourage you, not of random internet profiles who don't align with your mission and values. When done right, you'll connect with potential clients, readers, and business friends. You don't necessarily need a lot of people in your network, but you do need "real connections" with real people who want to see you succeed.

Don't know where to start? Here are some ways to discover new people on LinkedIn:

1. *Look for posts whose content you resonate with.* Follow those profiles, and notice who else is commenting on their posts.

2. *Find someone whose content is about a skill you'd like to learn* — for example, networking. Follow that person and see who else is commenting on their posts.

3. *Anytime you're on a group call, make note of who else is there.* If they seem like people you'd like to get to know, follow them or send them a connection request with a note that you are in the same group.

4. *Use LinkedIn's search filters to find specific types of profiles* — for example, life coaches, financial advisors, graphic designers, etc. Check out who shows up in the search results and follow those who look interesting to you.

5. *If someone you're not connected with makes a comment on your post*, follow them at first and send a connection request later if you like what you see on their page.

Your community will also enhance your visibility on the platform. The more they engage with your content — through reacting, commenting, and reposting — the more the algorithm will reward you with impressions, allowing you to reach more people and thus expand your network. Your core community can also offer you emotional support during your "chrysalis times" and when you're experimenting with new messaging, content formats, or paid offers.

You'll notice I am not recommending you connect with every single profile that you come across, and there's a reason for that. *Danielle Hughes* perfectly articulates when to simply follow versus when to go ahead and connect:

> *"Let's Talk About Connecting.* **Sending** someone a connection request on LinkedIn just so you can then follow up with an InMail to 'gently inquire' about their use of AI, systems, processes, lead gen, etc. IS NOT connecting. It's selling. And bad selling at that.
>
> I used to accept almost all requests on LinkedIn because the point of the platform is to connect. But lately I'm inundated with people who have 10X, 4X, $1M nonsense in their headlines.

Hot Tip: If you really want to see what I have to say, you can follow me. That's what the follow button is for. Connecting is for when you actually know me, want to read my content, or think I can truly benefit from yours.

Notice I said content, not services. Of course we're all here to grow our networks, our businesses, our expertise, and our revenue, but the only way to make that happen is through genuinely getting to know each other. And that takes time. And effort.

So while I appreciate people who want to connect with me, I'm now declining requests from people I don't know, don't have people in common with, and don't think will be valuable connections.

But they're welcome to follow me. For everyone else, I look forward to continuing to build meaningful relationships with you, learn from you, and help each other grow."[1]

So please, don't be one of those profile collectors. Show that you have a real, vested interest in the person when connecting with them. If you don't know how, take *Phil Gerbyshak's* advice:

> "*Serve First. Give First. Help First.* Networking isn't about getting something—it's about giving something.
>
> The most generous people always end up with the richest networks. Why? Because they become the go-to. The helper. The resource. The one who isn't trying to 'leverage' you but who shows up to lift you.
>
> Want to grow your network? Start with this question: What do I know, love, or care about that might help someone else today? Share that.
>
> Post a tip that solved a problem for you. Offer to help someone get unstuck. Leave a thoughtful comment, not just a 'like.' Make an introduction — with no expectation.
>
> You don't need a strategy deck. Just be useful."[2]

When "just a name" becomes a connection which then becomes a business relationship which ultimately becomes a friendship, it is priceless. Making friends is one of the best benefits of being on LinkedIn!

Here are five tips for connecting on LinkedIn and other social media platforms:

1. *Look for people you want to connect with.* Comment on their posts, attend their webinars, watch their LinkedIn Lives, listen to their podcasts, etc. Make a genuine connection with them by engaging with their content and showing that you're interested in what they have to say. Start to get to know the person behind the content

2. *Learn about a new skill.* Find someone whose content teaches a skill you want to learn more about (e.g., networking). Follow that person, check out their content, and comment on their posts. You'll start to uplevel your skill just by following that person's content.

3. *Send a DM.* When it feels right, send your new connection a DM (direct message) asking to have a 15-minute, no-agenda "coffee chat." Share about what you do as it comes up naturally in the conversation.

4. *Introduce people to each other when appropriate.* Be a referral source by introducing two people who could benefit from knowing each other.

5. *Meet up in real life when possible.* Meeting people in person creates an incredible bond not found online. I have been blessed to make some incredible real-life friendships, and they started out as just a name on LinkedIn.

Commenting

Leaving a positive comment on someone's post is so important because it makes that person feel seen, heard, and valued. Your words have the power to encourage someone whose self-esteem might be low that day. Your affirmation in a comment can temper self-doubt and increase self-confidence. You never know when sharing a kind word can make a huge difference for the person reading it. So remember: when commenting, be generous, be kind, give lots of praise, and highlight others.

Phil Gerbyshak has a beautiful way of explaining how I approach commenting:

> *"Let Generosity Do the Heavy Lifting.*
> The best part about all this?
>
> *When we teach and serve generously, networks take care of themselves.*
> That quote is everything.

You don't need to "network" in the traditional sense when you live this way. You'll attract people who align with your values. You'll stay top-of-mind not by shouting but by serving. You'll build a reputation that's based on being helpful, thoughtful, and kind — not slick, pushy, or polished.

That's not just how you build a network. It's how you build a legacy.

You Don't Need to Be 'Somebody' to Start.
You don't need a massive following. You don't need a bestselling book. You don't need a fancy job title.

You just need to show up with heart, share what you're learning, and help others do the same.

Because the people who teach and serve generously? They don't chase networks. Networks form around them."[3]

It's so important to remember that you don't have to feel "ready" in order to start building a community online.
You've got everything you need — even if you haven't published a single post yet, as *Mike Ashabraner* says:

"*The Psychology Behind Profitable Reciprocity.*
Here's why this works so well: when you give value first — whether through thoughtful comments, helpful introductions, or genuine support — you're demonstrating three powerful things:

1. You're not just talking about yourself all the time.
2. You're actually listening to what others have to say.
3. You're adding value to conversations others started.

This often creates a sort of psychological inclination to reciprocate that feels good rather than forced. It's not manipulation — it's human nature. It's one of the best ways to attract and repel the right and wrong folks for you and your business.

From Comments to Community.
Remember, your comments can actually build your community faster than your own posts alone ever will. While everyone else is shouting from their own digital front porch, smart community builders are quietly making friends in other folks' yards.

It's like the difference between throwing your own barbecue where you gotta convince folks to come versus showing up at the neighborhood potluck with the best dang apple pie anyone's ever tasted. Which one you reckon gets you more new friends?"[4]

Need more convincing? *Lynnaire Johnston* explains how important commenting is for visibility:

> "*Engagement Beats Posting.* Yes, really. Commenting is now the #1 visibility tactic. Why? Because LinkedIn has reduced the reach on our posts in favor of commercial content.
>
> Commenting on posts — particularly within the first hour — boosts your visibility across networks. It also improves reach on your own posts.
>
> And if you're tagged, always respond. Posting alone isn't enough anymore. It's your comments on others' content that get you noticed now. Make them count!"[5]

Finally, here are five tips for commenting on LinkedIn and other social media platforms:

1. *If you're not sure what to say when commenting, pretend you are already friends with that person.* To get past my fear of commenting on a stranger's post, I pretended we were already friends and commented as if we were. I psyched myself up to respond as if it were a friend's post — I simply had to ask myself, "What would I say to that friend?" The best part about using this tactic is that some of those people have become actual friends!

2. *Look for posts you like.* When I first joined LinkedIn, I knew very few people. In order to start commenting, I simply scrolled my feed, looking for posts that resonated with me.

3. *Find a sentence within the post that "speaks" to you.* Include that quote in your comment and tell the person why you like it, what it reminds you of, how it makes you feel, etc.

4. *Choose someone to compliment or celebrate.* This works best if the person is on LinkedIn so you can tag them, but they don't have to be in your network.

Also, make sure the compliment is genuine. It should come from the heart! Don't compliment for the sake of it — people can smell "fake" a mile away.

5. *Make a list of 10 potential clients and engage with them.* Establish a relationship by connecting with them and commenting on their posts. If you comment consistently, most people will notice. You are subtly calling attention to yourself *by keeping the focus on them* and opening the door to have a deeper one-on-one conversation.

Content

Creating content is another opportunity that allows you to soar, but in a different way. It gives people a chance to get to know who you are, what you believe, and what your message is.

Through your content, you can encourage, empower, inform, and enlighten others. Most importantly, you can make a "heart difference" by sharing your message. A "heart difference" is a message that will help someone else, making it transformational for that person. They receive value along with your kindness and compassion.

Your posts are a light for anyone who is battling self-doubt or who is too afraid to speak up. They are a beacon for your future readers and clients to identify *you* as the person to help them solve a problem. I said it at the beginning, but it's so important that it bears repeating: *someone is waiting to hear your message and will miss out on a transformation if you don't share it*!

Here are five tips for creating content on LinkedIn and other social media platforms:

1. *Consistency over quantity.* Post three times a week, two times a week, four times a week — whatever works for you. It doesn't have to be every day. Make a commitment to yourself to be consistent, however you define it.

2. *Respond to comments.* You'd be surprised how many people forget to do this or simply skip it. Always respond to every comment made on your posts. Acknowledge that they took the time to read your post and share their thoughts, and celebrate them for doing so!

3. *Keep track of ideas.* Struggling to come up with original content? Many of my posts are inspired by everyday life. Look for ideas and lessons in your day-to-day, and write them down. This practice will also help you narrow down what kind of content you want to create. What do you want to be known for?

4. *Include "business" and "personality" posts.* In between posting about your business and how you help people, sprinkle in "personality" posts. Share about your hobbies, your activities, your everyday happenings. Allow people to get to know YOU as a person.

5. *Create a post from one of your comments.* Use a comment you made on someone's post to create your own content. In your new post, expand on your original response.

> Bonus Tip: if you don't like to write, don't have time to write, or simply don't know what to write, you can outsource your content creation. Choose a content writer who will make sure the content is in your voice and whose topics are authentic to you.

Here are some social media tips from *Deborah Kevin*:

"Instead of the *spaghetti-on-the-wall* method (posting everywhere and hoping something sticks), try this:

Pick One or Two Platforms You Enjoy. You don't need to be on every platform. Start small. Get comfortable. Then consider expanding.

Create a Content Rhythm You Can Maintain. Think weekly, not daily. Use scheduling tools. Repurpose content across platforms.

Engage, Don't Just Broadcast. Comment on posts, respond to messages, and build relationships. You're not a billboard. You're a person.

Be Generous with Value. Offer writing tips, behind-the-scenes insights, your favorite reads, or just honest reflections. Show people what it's like inside your creative world.

Set Boundaries. Decide how much time you want to spend on social media and stick to it. Protect your writing time like it's sacred. Because it is."[6]

Your Social Media Impact Trifecta

Strategic connecting, commenting, and content are ALL needed to turn your LinkedIn efforts into clients.

Look for people you want to connect with or who post about a skill you want to learn. Invite them to have a "coffee chat" to get to know each other. If you're not sure what to say in the comments, pretend you are already friends with that person. Look for posts you like and leave a thoughtful comment about what resonates with you and why. Post consistently and respond to people who comment on your content. Finally, include both "business" and "personality" topics in your content.

This combination is important because it's the best way to create a community of potential clients and business friends. Together, the 3Cs of the Butterfly Strategy help you make an impact, inspire connections, and increase your visibility while allowing you to share about your message and who you are as a person outside of business too.

THINK ABOUT

- Who do I really want in my LinkedIn community — people who become business friends, potential clients, readers, mentors, coaches, or [fill in the blank]?
- Which do I want to focus on more: real relationships or lots of contacts?
- What impression do I want someone to have after seeing my LinkedIn profile?
- In what ways can I support people?
- How do I want people to feel after they interact with me on LinkedIn?

TO DO

Pick one tip to do from each section (Connecting, Commenting, and Content Creation).

Here are activities to help you start creating your community on LinkedIn through *Connecting* and *Commenting*:

1. Make a list of 10 people you'd like to know better. Start following them.
2. Of those 10 people choose two people each day to comment on their posts. (Make meaningful comments that are at least 15 words in length.)

Continued...

3. After following these 10 people for two weeks, choose one each week to send a warm, personalized connection request to.
4. Each week, ask one connection for a "virtual coffee chat" as a way to get to know them better.
5. Find an event (webinar, masterclass, etc) to attend on LinkedIn and choose at least one or two people to interact with at that event.

Here are activities to help with *Content Creation*:

Choose to post twice a week — one business post and one personality post.

Choose what kind of content you want to focus on first: building trust, sharing stories, or celebrating others.

Share something new that you've learned this week. (If it's from someone who is also on LinkedIn, mention their name and tag them in the post.)

Create a post from of your comments on someone else's post. Expand on your comment.

Respond to every comment made on your own posts with a thoughtful response of your own. (Your comments are a form of content.)

PART 2

Content Creation

By now, you know that the best way to leverage the Butterfly Strategy is to focus on the combination of connecting, commenting, and content creation. Depending on your stage of business, you might be tempted to outsource some or all of the 3Cs. Before you do, know this: to get the most out of your social media presence, *you* need to be the one connecting and commenting.

Yes, there are service providers who will post and comment for you. But I strongly believe that if you have a social media presence, you need to be *present*. Here's why: if you let someone else comment for you, they could never replicate your authenticity. If you then meet one of your new connections on a Zoom call, they may be basing their opinion of you, in part, on your comments on their posts and on others'. If you weren't the one personally leaving those comments, it could give that new connection the wrong impression about you.

That said, the one area that can be outsourced is content creation — *if* you find a copywriter or content writer who will create content that is authentic to *you*, in your voice, using your words.

Part 2 focuses on content creation. These ideas apply whether you are creating your own content or asking a copywriter or content writer to do it for you. First, we'll look at creating an article. (At first glance, you might not like the sound of creating an article, but I will show you how useful it can be for your LinkedIn presence — think repurposing!) Then, I'll give you content ideas with examples so you can get started on posts right away.

Creating an Article

Why an Article?

When you think about content creation for LinkedIn, what comes to mind? I'm willing to bet you're thinking about posts. Do you really have to write articles too? Are articles even relevant anymore? My answer is YES!

Writing a LinkedIn article is still worth it, especially when you use it as the basis for even more content. An effective way to leverage your expertise is to write an article and then repurpose it into LinkedIn posts. Not only is this strategy a built-in way to post consistently on LinkedIn, but it also helps foster connection and credibility, positioning you as the expert.

Additionally, if your followers tend to ask the same questions over and over again, that's your cue to write an article which will act as pillar content for your audience. The next time someone asks you that same question, you can refer them to the article. Plus, some articles hosted on LinkedIn (as of this writing) are showing up in Google and AI searches. Hello, visibility!

Let's go a little more into detail about why writing an article is a smart move for your business.

Establish Yourself as the Expert

Does your target market — the people you want to do business with — know you exist? How are you telling them about the service or product you offer? For your ideal clients to want to contact you, they need to know who you are and how you will solve their problem.

Writing a LinkedIn article is a smart way to share your expertise. Not only does an article give value to your target market, but it also positions you as the resource, the go-to person, to solve their problem.

This is the power of thought leadership content — you don't sound like a derivative of someone else because you are sharing about your lived experiences and your previous clients' results. You don't even have to worry about having the perfect graphics or professional headshots. You just have to write about what you know best.

It's time for YOU to be quoted in an article as the expert!

Two Main Benefits: Time and Consistency

Other than establishing yourself as the expert, two main benefits of writing an article are leveraging your *time* and creating *consistency* in your content calendar. How do you do that? By repurposing the article into posts.

Consider this equation:
1 Article + Leverage + Repurpose =
8 Impactful LinkedIn Content Posts

For example, let's say you post twice weekly. Writing just one article will give you four weeks' worth of content with an overall coordinated theme. So instead of writing eight posts on different topics, you can write just one longer article on the same topic. From there, you can simply pull out excerpts from your article and use them as posts.

You'll spend less time writing when you start with long-form pillar content and repurpose it into micro content.

Now that you don't have to come up with new ideas for posts anymore, you can publish them even more consistently than before. Why does consistency matter? Because when you're present on LinkedIn on a regular basis, you're viewed as credible, trustworthy, and familiar. And as a bonus, the algorithm will reward you with higher reach when you consistently show up and give value.

Previously, I mentioned that content is the only one of the 3Cs I recommend outsourcing. If you're wondering whether it makes sense for you to outsource your content, consider:

- Do you spend more than two hours a month writing content for LinkedIn posts when your time could be better served doing other activities for your business?
- Would you rather talk on a podcast than write a post? Do you self-sabotage because you want every post to be perfect?

If you answered yes to any of these, consider hiring a copywriter or content writer. The time you save on content creation can then be reallocated — whether to your business or to yourself.

Choosing the Topic for Your Article

Let's say you're still writing all your own content. Even though you no longer have to come up with ideas for new posts, you still have to determine the topic for an article. If you're struggling here, think about what your ideal client needs to know. Focus on solving a problem they have right now.

Follow these steps to identify the topic of your first article:

1. Brainstorm what you want your potential clients to know about. Write down any and all ideas you can come up with in 10 minutes.

2. From the list, pick out the top three ideas — the ones that will give the most value to your client.

3. For each of the three ideas, answer these questions:

    - If you could sit down face-to-face with your client, what would you say to them about this issue?

- What are the three main points about this issue that your client needs to know?
- How can you solve their problem? What solution(s) do you offer?
- What questions are you often asked relating to this issue?
- How can you provide value for your client?
- How can you positively impact this client?
- How can you show yourself as the expert, as the go-to person, as the resource for solving the client's problem?

4. Choose one of the top three ideas as the topic for your first article.

Remember to leverage your article: not only can you re-purpose the content for social media posts, but you can also add it to your website, the Featured section on your LinkedIn page, your newsletter, or your blog.

Five Post Ideas with Examples

For posts, you might not always be repurposing articles, especially in the case of personality posts. To get you started on standalone posts, here are my five favorite content creation ideas anyone can use.

1 | The Origin Story

What is your origin story? Telling your "origin story" (or "backstory") is an essential component of your content strategy. Don't let the name fool you — it's not an epic saga. Origin story content simply tells how you got to where you are today.

Usually it's about how you once struggled with the same obstacles as your target clients before you achieved the transformation they're seeking. It's okay to be vulnerable in sharing about what you went through. Overcoming adversity is powerful — and relatable. People want to know how you solved that problem. If not for any other reason, then share your origin story because it might help someone else on their way to transformation.

A "Business Spotlight" or an "Author Spotlight" is another way to share your origin story. Write about how the business started or how the idea for the book came about.

You're presenting solutions and sharing some background that many will be able to relate to.

Origin Story Example:

> *It was as if it was giving approval of the tiny human I was holding...*

March + September + Monarch = Hope

A monarch seemed to almost kiss me and my two-week-old granddaughter, lingering for a few seconds by us before flying up to a nearby tree. Amidst the sunshine on this fall day, it fluttered in the leaves and then disappeared.

It was as if it was giving approval of the tiny human I was holding in my arms.

We were sitting on the deck, watching her twin brothers play outside. As it flew out of my sight, I immediately thought of my dad.

March 2018 – We very unexpectedly had to say goodbye to my dad, as he wasn't able to overcome a brain bleed.

September 2018 – Life was being celebrated again with the birth of my granddaughter.

Later that afternoon, the boys and I were walking by a vacant lot when a monarch flew right by us. It paused on a dandelion long enough for me to take a picture. Again — I thought of my dad.

I call it my "butterfly of hope" because I believe it was sent twice that day to help me remember that there is still hope and love in this world.

This butterfly reminded me that I need to continue the legacy my dad left me.

I'm using "butterfly" in my business name as a reminder to share the values of hope and love with others — just like my dad did. He left a tremendous legacy, and I want to do the same.

2 | The Parable

What's a parable? One of the best ways to connect with people is to evoke an *emotion*. And one of the best ways to evoke an emotion is to tell a parable: a simple story that illustrates a powerful lesson. For example, share an experience that has impacted you or changed you. Everyone has a story like this to share.

Stories are powerful and relatable — so share your heart and let others see what has made a difference in your life.

Parable Example:

> *The last three items on his birthday wish list were unexpected...*
>
> Four-year-old Ryder found a #4 candle in the cupboard. This prompted him to ask for a cake for his fifth birthday — even though it was months away.
>
> His mommy wisely didn't argue but told him to make a list and that they would go shopping later.

Thrilled, he found a piece of paper and a red crayon and proceeded to make his list.

He knew his letters, and he knew what he wanted to put on the list — he just needed help with spelling the words. So he asked for my help.

The first three items on the list were expected: sugar, cake mix, and balloons. Because those words took the whole page, he flipped it over to continue

The list on the second page, however, wasn't expected: he included wishes from his heart that brought tears to my eyes. I swallowed the lump in my throat as I spelled the words he asked for: someone, lots, love.

With a huge smile on his face, he exclaimed, "I want lots of someones to come to my party! I love them!"

And with a heartfelt hug, I agreed with him. I took pictures of his "birthday cake list" to remind myself and others what we all really need: someone to share love with.

Heart wishes from a child are like a huge celebration. They honor the essence of life: having "love" and "someone" — and "lots" of both!

3 | Question & Answer

The question-and-answer format is straightforward. In case you're still short of ideas, here are three you can use as a jumping off point:

- What are your clients' most-asked questions? Answering a question in a post is a smart way to help more than one person at a time.
- Did you find a journal prompt that really intrigued you? Share your thoughts on how you answered it.
- Is there a topic you would like to share? Create a question about it and then give your answer.

Q & A Example:

What are some ways to make genuine connections?

A first step is to look for people you want to connect with. It's *people* who make the difference!

When looking for people to connect with on LinkedIn, be open, kind, friendly, and willing to meet people who aren't exactly like you because you never know who might know someone who you can help or who can help you!

Once the connection is made, be genuine. Start to get to know them as a person — do *not* start selling to them!

The benefit of establishing a relationship is that this "connection" could become a client, a referral, a resource, or best of all — a friend (business or personal)!

Find someone who is sharing a skill you want to learn more about (e.g., networking).

When it feels right, send that person a DM (direct message) asking to have a 15-minute "coffee chat" — but with no agenda.

Meet people in real life when possible.

Create a genuine connection so it can lead to a relationship which may lead to a friendship — business or personal! One of the best reasons for being on LinkedIn is to create a community of clients and *business friends*. Friends know who you are and what you do, and can refer you to others.

4 | Turn Your Comment Into a Post

Commenting is already part of your social media strategy, so why not leverage your comments and turn them into posts? Plus, it's original content, so you're still positioning yourself as the expert without having to come up with yet another idea for a post.

All you have to do is write meaningful responses to other people's posts. When you make a comment that you think is particularly valuable or conversation-worthy, take those words and expand on them to create a post of your own.

It's good practice to reference the original post and tag that person, but focus on your authentic message. Share *your* thoughts on the topic in *your* words.

Turn Your Comment Into a Post Example:

Stuff or a memory?

What is your favorite kind of gift to give?

People are 3x more likely to feel long-lasting gratitude for *experiential* purchases than for *material* things. (Scott Boddie)

For me, I think investing quality time with someone is one of the best gifts to give.

Content Creation

As my grandblessings are getting older, I decided to stop giving "stuff" that they will probably only play with for a short time. Instead, I am choosing to give them the "gift of experience or memories."

This includes a "birthday date" and a "Christmas date." What that means is that I take each one individually to the restaurant of his/her choice. It may also include a movie or some other activity. One-on-one time gives me the opportunity to focus solely on each child without the other children in the family vying for my attention.

I want this tradition to create positive memories so that the time spent with me will last long after the "stuff" is gone.

This is important to me because it gives me the opportunity to create a special connection or bond with each one. I want to create cherished relationships — especially with my little ones — and giving the gift of time/memories is one of the best ways for me to do that.

5 | Gratitude Reflection

A gratitude reflection is perfect for a post because it touches the soul and makes a "heart difference" in a special way.

Sharing a gratitude list makes your post original and genuine because it's about what *you* are grateful for. Write from the heart and then start a conversation with others about what you have in common.

Even if your list only contains aspects of everyday life, it will still make an impact with readers because focusing on gratitude is life-changing!

Gratitude Reflection Example:

> *Startling statistic:* The average person's thoughts are approximately 60—80% negative.
>
> What made me think of that statistic again was a meme I saw that said:
>
> "Did you know? You can 'rewire' your brain to be happy by simply recalling three things you're grateful for every day for 21 days." (Author unknown)

I'd rather focus on happy thoughts than on negative ones.

Kevin Bailey explained it this way: "Several studies have shown that the average person's thoughts are approximately 60 to 80% negative. So a gratitude practice focuses the brain on firing and strengthening the other 20% to 40% of neural networks that lean positive."

That had me thinking a lot about gratitude and how I could make my thoughts more positive rather than negative.

I decided to start with one simple thing — washing dishes — and think of some ways to be grateful because of it.

** I am thankful we had food and thankful for the farmers who grew the food.
** I am thankful for dirty dishes because that meant we had food to eat.

** I am thankful for clean water to wash the dishes with.
** I am thankful the water heater was working so I could have warm water in the sink.
** I am thankful for the lavender scent of the dish soap.

That "negative thoughts statistic" really bothers me, so I am going to try to focus on being grateful for more of the everyday things in my life — things I take for granted (like dirty dishes) — to "rewire my brain" and increase my gratitude.

What is one simple thing you are grateful for today? Or what is one way you can increase your gratitude practice?

Bonus: Personify Your Business

This is a fun one: create a post that describes your business as if it were a person!

First, give your "business person" a name. Then, ask yourself:

- What personality traits do you have relating to the services you offer? What character traits?
- What is your gift to others?

Personify Your Business Example:

If my business were a person, here is how I would describe her...

Meet "Victoria"! Her passion is writing and helping people succeed by sharing their message.

She realizes that not everyone has time to write or likes to write, but she does! Writing lights her up! She loves to highlight people, sharing how they are serving others.

Victoria's gift: helping people save time and decrease stress, allowing them to soar above content creation roadblocks — especially when writing is hard or not fun for them to do. She loves being their "content creation partner writer" and creating authentic, impactful content just for them.

Her mission: to help people shine through writing, helping them make an impact and build a community of *business friends*, readers, and clients.

THINK ABOUT...
- How much time do you spend on content creation for LinkedIn each month?
- Could that time be better spent doing something else and you hire a copywriter or content writer to create your LinkedIn content?
- Are you showing up authentically on LinkedIn?
- Does your content truly reflect who you are and what your values are?
- What questions do clients ask you that could be answered in a post or article?
- Do you want to be considered a "thought leader" or a "participant" on LinkedIn?
- How would your business change if people consistently saw you as the *go-to expert* in your field?

TO DO...

Choose one of the five content topic examples (above) and create a post.

Brainstorm what you want your potential clients to know about. Write down all of the ideas you can come up with in 10 minutes.

From the list, pick out the top three ideas — the ones that will give the most value to your client.

Choose one of the top three ideas as the topic for your first article.

Write a first draft — or find someone who can write in *your voice* to create the article for you.

WHEN TO CONSIDER OUTSOURCING YOUR CONTENT:

- How much time do you currently spend on content creation?
- Is it the best use of your time and energy — or could it be better spent doing some other activity that helps you grow your business?
- Do you have articles in which you are quoted as the go-to expert?
- Do your articles and posts sound professional and represent you authentically? Do you like the message they are giving?
- Are you missing opportunities because you aren't sharing your expertise consistently online?
- Do you enjoy writing or would you rather do something else?
- Could a professional writer express your ideas more clearly?

PART 3

Butterfly Strategy Principles

By now, you understand that you need to strategically connect, comment, and create content in order to maximize the benefits of being on LinkedIn.

In this final section, let's explore — in keeping with the butterfly theme — five principles that explain why creating authentic content is so important.

Your Proverbial Scales

Consider the butterfly. We see stunning colors, but their wings are actually transparent. The colors come from the light reflecting off tiny scales on their wings.

Your content needs proverbial scales. Don't force the colors — be reflective of who you really are. Be transparent. Be genuine. Authentic content does not mean over-revealing or appearing perfect. Focus on making your personality and your message shine through.

Create a content strategy that captures your voice and your values so that you can avoid sounding generic and so that you will show up consistently with content that shares your message.

Your Content Diet

A butterfly can't live off sugar alone, so it will sometimes sip from a mud puddle which contains minerals and salts to supplement its diet.

Just like butterflies can't rely only on flowers for their nutritional needs, relying strictly on inspiration for great content usually doesn't work. Your content diet needs a combination of "sugar, minerals, and salt" — meaning you need to share about:

- yourself ("sugar"),
- your book and your message ("minerals"),
- and how you can make a difference for others ("salt").

If getting enough "sugar, minerals, and salt" in your content diet is holding you back from sharing impactful, consistent posts, find someone to brainstorm nutrient-rich ideas with. Your brainstorming buddy will help decrease frustration and stress, and eliminate the overwhelm of what to say.

Flying "Cold"

The cold prevents a butterfly from flying. "Cold content" prevents your message from resonating with your target audience.

Just as the air temperature affects a butterfly's ability to function, if you're overwhelmed about showing up on LinkedIn, that affects your ability to share your message... and results in you not posting consistently or posting information just for the sake of it — but it isn't really what you want to share about.

Maybe you don't know what you really want to share about in the first place! Or maybe you know what you want to share about, but you're afraid to post it. Or you have lots of ideas and aren't afraid to post them, but you don't have time to write.

Waiting for a huge block of time to create, waiting for inspiration, or waiting for AI to save you usually doesn't make for the kind of content that positively highlights you.

When the butterfly is cold, it can't fly until it has warmed up. If your LinkedIn content is "cold," you need a way to "warm" it up. Don't stay in flight-or-freeze mode. Create a system that allows you to show up consistently and to genuinely share your message.

Making Time

After emerging from its cocoon, the butterfly must pump fluids into its wings before it is strong enough to fly.

The same is true for your content. Expecting to come up with ideas simply through "inspiration," or thinking that time will magically appear, probably won't happen. Instead, create a strategy with intentional ideas that really reflect who you are and what your message is.

A strategy allows you to work smarter because you'll have content created, taking the pressure off relying on inspiration or trying to find extra time. A strategy allows you to *manufacture* inspiration and *make* time — your ideas can emerge from the cocoon and become strong because the content is authentic to you.

Your Ultraviolet Message

When you don't know what to write about, a blank screen can be intimidating. You sit there, waiting for inspiration to strike... and after a great deal of overthinking, and no words appearing, you shut down your computer and walk away. Frustrated. Stressed. No post. No progress... just wasted time.

Are you forcing an idea that doesn't fit who you are or what your message is? Are you trying to share about something that doesn't authentically relate to you? You may not know what to focus on for your content, but your special message is still there — it's just waiting to be discovered and shared.

A butterfly is nearsighted, but one of its special powers is being able to see ultraviolet colors that are invisible to the human eye. The ability to see these certain colors allows the butterfly to know which direction to go.

You have the same kind of superpower — you have valuable insights that will give people direction. But you need to share them! Instead of waiting for inspiration to land or trying to force an idea that only leads to frustration, consider tapping into a process that helps you bring out your stories, your insights, and your value.

Create content that focuses on the "colors" of your distinct message. The butterfly uses its superpower to find the next flower — you can do the same.

Choose to Be a Butterfly by Using Your Transformation Superpowers!

If I could choose only one word to describe the message of this book, it would be *Community*!

It's essential to build a community of people — readers, potential clients, and business friends — who will support and encourage you! When sharing your message, your book, your course, your membership, whatever it is, you'll need your community.

That community should be built on genuine relationships. You need to nurture your connections to become business friendships. One way to start doing that is through commenting on other people's posts and responding to comments on your posts. Then follow up with real conversations.

And while content is important, it only matters *after* you've connected with someone who is looking to see what you're sharing about, what your values are, what you believe.

Choose to be a butterfly. Emerge from the cocoon believing in yourself, ask others to help you become strong, and then take flight, aiming to serve others.

A butterfly shows us what transformation looks like. We can create a transformation, too.

Remember: strategic connecting, commenting, and content creation are your transformation superpowers to help you make the biggest impact. That's the essence of the Butterfly Strategy — may it help you to soar and serve others!

I wish you much success — in however you define it — with an abundance of light, hope, love, and genuine relationships.

PART 4

Glossary of Terms

The following terms are listed in the order they appear in the book.

Community: A community is the people who will support and encourage you. Build a community of people who become business friends, potential clients, and readers.

Business Friend: A business friend is someone you meet online or in-person who will support and encourage you. While some may become clients, most will not, but can be resources or referral sources for you. A business friend will amplify your voice and celebrate you.

Connect: Find people to meet who can become business friends. Connect with them through a conversation and start getting to know who they are.

Commenting: Leave your thoughts on other people's posts as well as responding to comments on your posts. Commenting can lead to conversations.

Content: What you post gives people a glimpse of who you are, what you believe, what your values are. Who/what do you want to be known for? Your content shares your message, letting people know how you can help them.

Virtual Coffee Chat: Setting up an online call to spend a few minutes getting to know a person — meeting them for the first time and just talking with them — NO pitching!

Algorithm: The behind-the-scenes system that determines what posts people see on LinkedIn.

Social Media Presence: How you choose to appear on social media.

Transformation: When you share your message via connecting, commenting, and content, you are inspiring people to act. You hare helping them change for the better. You are helping people to make a positive impact.

Glossary of Terms

Social Media Strategy: A strategy for social media is a plan with intentional ideas that really reflect who you are and what your message is. It allows you to work smarter because you have content created, taking the pressure off relying on "inspiration" or finding that "extra time." A strategy helps you to stop wasting your limited time and attention.

Business Posts: Business posts are content that shares about whom you serve and how you can help them.

Personality Posts: Personality posts are content about yourself outside of the business sphere. Share about your favorite activity or hobby. People want to know who you are.

Social Media Impact Trifecta: While connecting, commenting, and posting content are each important individual actions in your social media strategy, it's the strategic combination of all three that creates the biggest impact — transforming your efforts into a community of potential clients, readers, and business friends. This is your Social Media Impact Trifecta!

Heart Difference: A "heart difference" is a message that will help someone else, making it transformational for that person. They receive value along with your kindness and compassion.

Article: An article in which you are the one being quoted helps to foster connection and credibility, positioning you as the expert.

Target Market: Your target market is the people you want to do business with.

Acknowledgments

While I have heard this before, I now know it to be absolutely true: it takes a village to create a book!

Special thanks to:

Ilise Benun and Lisa Mullis
Thank you for believing in me. Your coaching and mentoring shaped my business to help people shine through writing. Your support and encouragement have been most appreciated!

Jessica Andersen
Your Brand Book coaching and manuscript editing have been invaluable! I wouldn't have made it to the finish line without your insight, encouragement, and assistance.

Dianne Volek
After learning so much from you on LinkedIn, I am now benefiting from your incredible expertise in book publishing and promotion. I am thankful for the wealth of knowledge you are sharing with me!

Toni Serofin

When you agreed to design my book cover and interior layout, I was excited! I'm pleased with the final look, thanks to your amazing expertise. Because of you, I met Jessica and Dianne. (And because of you three, I have a book which I am proud of — and I am so thankful for this dream becoming a reality!)

Jesus Christ, my Savior

I am grateful to Jesus for giving me a passion for writing, and for guiding me through this process and through life.

About the Author

Val Roskens Tews is a content strategy writer for small business owners, coaches, and authors who want to grow their audience and attract clients without getting stuck in the overwhelm of what to post or how to say it. Through her Butterfly Strategy and Conversation to Content methods, Val helps clients go from scattered ideas to a clear, authentic presence online. With a background in journalism and public relations, her work weaves together strategy, storytelling, and heart, so her clients build meaningful relationships, show up consistently, and create communities that care. Her approach is warm, intuitive, and designed to help people find more clarity and confidence with their content.

She believes in the power of small, thoughtful actions — like connecting, commenting, and creating — to create ripple effects of trust, visibility, and opportunity across social platforms. Val's goal is simple: to help people share their message with less stress and more joy, one conversation — and one piece of content — at a time.

Connect with Val:

LinkedIn: https://www.linkedin.com/in/val-roskens-tews
Email: val@butterflycopywriting.com

Endnotes

1 Danielle Hughes, LinkedIn post. https://www.linkedin.com/posts/daniellehughes_lets-talk-about-connecting-sending-someone-activity-7345801196470763521-bbY7/

2 Phil Gerbyshak, *Build a Network Without Feeling Slimy: Teach, Serve, and Show Up Where People Are.* https://www.linkedin.com/pulse/build-network-without-feeling-slimy-teach-serve-show-up-gerbyshak-g8lnc/

3 Phil Gerbyshak, *Build a Network Without Feeling Slimy: Teach, Serve, and Show Up Where People Are.* https://www.linkedin.com/pulse/build-network-without-feeling-slimy-teach-serve-show-up-gerbyshak-g8lnc/

4 Mike Ashabraner, *Counterintuitive Networking Approach that Fills Your Calendar Without Pitching.* https://www.linkedin.com/pulse/counterintuitive-networking-approach-fills-your-mike-ashabraner-jjquc/

5. Lynnaire Johnston, *Job Searching on LinkedIn: Everything You've Been Missing.* https://www.linkedin.com/pulse/job-searching-linkedin-everything-youve-been-missing-johnston-bvaac/

6. Deborah Kevin, *Is It Necessary to Post on Social Media as an Author?* https://debbykevin.substack.com/p/the-role-of-social-media-in-book

www.ingramcontent.com/pod-product-compliance
Lightning Source LLC
Chambersburg PA
CBHW041038050426
42337CB00058B/4986